BIOGRAPHIES

AMELIA
EARHART

by Erika L. Shores

PEBBLE
a capstone imprint

Pebble Explore is published by Pebble, an imprint of Capstone.
1710 Roe Crest Drive
North Mankato, Minnesota 56003
www.capstonepub.com

**Library of Congress Cataloging-in-Publication Data is available on the
Library of Congress website.**
ISBN: 978-1-9771-2329-9 (hardcover)
ISBN: 978-1-9771-2654-2 (paperback)
ISBN: 978-1-9771-2337-4 (eBook PDF)

Summary:
How much do you know about Amelia Earhart? Find out the facts you need
to know about this female aviator. You'll learn about the early life, challenges,
and major accomplishments of this important American.

Image Credits
Alamy: Science History Images, 15; AP Photo: 21, 25; Bridgeman Images:
16; Courtesy of Purdue University Libraries, Karnes Archives and Special
Collections: 22; Getty Images: Authenticated News, 6, Bettmann, 7, 18, 26,
Corbis/George Rinhart, 11, FPG, 8; Granger: 13; Library of Congress: 5, 29,
National Child Labor Committee Collection, 9; Newscom: Album, cover, 1,
Everett Collection, 17; Shutterstock: Alex Landa (geometric background),
cover, back cover, 2, 29, Everett Historical, 19, Sharon Day, 27

Editorial Credits
Editor: Anna Butzer; Designer: Elyse White; Media Researcher: Svetlana
Zhurkin; Production Specialist: Spencer Rosio

Printed in the United States
PO117

The author dedicates this book to Chris German.

Table of Contents

Words in **bold** are in the glossary.

Who Was Amelia Earhart?

Amelia Earhart was **brave**. She was a **pilot**. Airplanes were new in the early 1900s. Few people were pilots. And very few pilots were women. Amelia did things no other woman had done before. She flew an airplane alone across oceans.

People all over the world knew about Amelia. Amelia had big dreams. She wanted to fly around the world. Sadly, she did not finish her trip. She and her plane went missing. People still want to know what happened to Amelia. She has not been forgotten.

Childhood

Amelia Mary Earhart was born July 24, 1897. Her parents were Amy and Edwin Earhart. Amelia's sister, Muriel, was born two and a half years later. The sisters were born in Atchison, Kansas. Their father worked for the railroad.

Amelia's family lived in this house in Atchison, Kansas.

Amelia (right) and Muriel

The family moved a lot for Edwin's job. Growing up, Amelia and Muriel lived in Kansas, Iowa, Minnesota, and Illinois. Amelia and Muriel were very close.

Amelia in 1904

In Amelia's time, boys could play rough games. But girls were to wear dresses and stay inside. Amy Earhart wanted her girls to enjoy animals and spend time outside. The Earhart sisters rode horses. They climbed trees. They played sports. Amelia liked basketball.

Amelia had a lot of ideas. She saw a roller coaster at a fair. She wanted to make her own. She and Muriel found a box and wood for the rails. Amelia took the first ride. She crashed and hurt her lip. But she told Muriel it felt as if she were flying.

People riding a roller coaster in Cincinnati, Ohio, in 1908

When she wasn't playing outside, Amelia read books. She and her sister took turns reading out loud to each other. One sister read while the other washed dishes or cleaned.

Amelia liked school. She was good at math and science. She finished high school in 1915, in Chicago, Illinois. Then she moved to Pennsylvania to go to **boarding school**. She did not finish this school. Amelia had visited her sister in Toronto, Canada. She decided to move there.

Amelia posed for a school photo in 1918.

Becoming Amelia

Amelia worked as a nurse's helper in a hospital in Toronto. This was during World War I (1914–1918). People first used airplanes during this war. Amelia took care of hurt pilots. She went to the nearby airfield. She talked to the pilots. She loved to see the airplanes.

After the war ended, Amelia decided to become a doctor. But soon after starting at Columbia University, Amelia changed her mind. She left college and moved to California. Her parents lived there at the time.

Amelia was working as a nurse's aid in 1918.

Taking Flight

In California, Amelia took her first airplane ride. She knew right away that she wanted to fly, herself.

Amelia got a job at a telephone company. She used the money she made to pay for flying lessons. A woman pilot named Neta Snook taught Amelia how to fly.

Amelia and her first
airplane in 1921

In 1921, Amelia bought an airplane.
It was bright yellow. She named it
The Canary.

In the early 1920s, very few women were licensed pilots.

In 1922, Amelia set a flying **record**. She was the first woman to fly at 14,000 feet (4,267 meters). A year later, Amelia got her pilot's **license**. She was the 16th woman to earn a pilot's license.

Amelia rode along on a flight across the Atlantic Ocean in 1928. She was the first woman to cross the ocean in an airplane. Then she wrote a book about the trip. The book was titled *20 Hrs. 40 Min.* That was how long the flight lasted.

Amelia with her airplane in 1928

In 1929, Amelia flew in an all-women's air race. She came in third place. Later that year, she and other women pilots started a group called The Ninety-Nines. They wanted more women to fly.

Several members of The Ninety-Nines in 1935 (Amelia not pictured)

Amelia after her solo flight in 1932

Amelia married George Putnam in 1931. George was a book publisher. He wanted Amelia to keep flying.

Amelia flew a plane **solo** across the Atlantic Ocean in 1932. She was the first woman and the second person to ever make this trip.

Amelia became famous. She wrote books and gave speeches all over the world.

In 1935, Amelia became the first person to fly solo across the Pacific Ocean. She was then the only person who had flown solo across both the Pacific and Atlantic Oceans.

21

Amelia (left) sitting on top of her
Lockheed Electra with a group
of Purdue students in 1936

Amelia went to work for Purdue University in 1935. She talked about the science of flying. She told female students about jobs they could get.

With the school's help, Amelia got a new airplane. It was a Lockheed Electra. She started to think about flying around the world. No pilot had ever done that.

On June 1, 1937, Amelia set off to fly around the world. Fred Noonan joined Amelia. His job was to read maps. He helped Amelia know where to fly.

They had completed 22,000 miles (35,405 kilometers) of their trip by July 2. Amelia and Fred took off from New Guinea that day. They were headed to Howland Island in the Pacific Ocean. But they never made it. People on ships searched in the area for Amelia and Fred for 16 days before giving up.

Amelia Earhart and Fred Noonan in 1937

Remembering Amelia Earhart

People still want to know what happened to Amelia, Fred, and the plane. They look for signs of the plane. In 2019, a group used special tools to search underwater. But the group did not solve the mystery. The story of Amelia's final flight remains unknown.

Amelia and Fred with a map that shows their planned route around the world

Amelia Earhart Birthplace Museum

Today people can visit Amelia's birthplace in Kansas. Many books have been written about her life and final flight. Amelia is remembered as an important leader for women. She wanted the world to know women could do anything men could do.

Important Dates

July 24, 1897	Amelia Earhart is born in Atchison, Kansas.
1915	Amelia finishes high school.
1916	Amelia enters the Ogontz School near Philadelphia, Pennsylvania.
1918	Amelia works at Spadina Military Hospital in Toronto, Canada.
1919	Amelia enters college at Columbia University in New York.
January 1921	Amelia takes her first flying lessons from Neta Snook.
July 1921	Amelia buys her first airplane.
1929	Amelia helps organize The Ninety-Nines.
1932	Amelia becomes the first woman to fly solo across the Atlantic Ocean.
1935	Amelia becomes the first person to fly solo across the Pacific Ocean; she is the first person to fly solo across both the Atlantic and Pacific Oceans.
June 1, 1937	Amelia and Fred Noonan attempt to fly around the world.
July 2, 1937	Amelia's plane goes missing.

Fast Facts

Name:
Amelia Earhart

Role:
pilot

Life dates:
Amelia was born July 24, 1897. She went missing July 2, 1937. Her death was made official on January 5, 1939.

Key accomplishments:
Amelia Earhart was the first woman to fly across the Atlantic Ocean. She was the first person to fly across the Pacific Ocean.

Glossary

brave (BRAYV)—showing courage and willingness to do difficult things

boarding school (BOR-ding SKOOL)—a school where students live during the school year

license (LYE-suhnss)—a document that officially makes it okay to do something

pilot (PYE-luht)—a person who flies a jet or plane

record (REK-urd)—when something is done better than anyone has ever done it before

solo (SOH-lo)—to do something alone

Read More

Meltzer, Brad. *I Am Unstoppable: A Little Book About Amelia Earhart*. New York: Dial Books for Young Readers, 2019.

Thiel, Kristin. *Amelia Earhart: First Woman to Fly Solo Across the Atlantic*. New York: Cavendish Square Publishing, 2018.

Weakland, Mark. *When Amelia Earhart Built a Roller Coaster*. North Mankato, MN: Picture Window Books, 2017.

Internet Sites

Amelia Earhart Birthplace Museum
www.ameliaearhartmuseum.org/

Amelia Earhart Collection
collections.lib.purdue.edu/aearhart/index.php

One Life: Amelia Earhart
npg.si.edu/exhibit/earhart/index.html

Index